Inquiries should be addressed to:

Afrodemiks@gmail.com

Library of Congress Cataloging-Publication Data is available.

ISBN10: 0692376224
ISBN 13: 9780693376225

Author April Thomas
Illustrator Cory Lampkin Jr.

Author's Notes

Here's a little poem dedicated to YOU!!

I hope you enjoy this book and share with family too.

You are the reason I do what I do.

Your beautiful smiles and cute little faces.

Continue to make the right choices and you'll go places.

So dream big and think far.

You are a shining star.

Always know you can achieve.

All you have to do is look in the mirror and just believe!!

Dedication

I dedicated this book to the extraordinary educators that have guided me

along the way throughout my college career and the journey of creating

this masterpiece:

Dr. Betty Porter Walls

Dr. Reynaldo Anderson

Mrs. Dorothy Turner

Mrs. Tracie Berry-McGhee

Mrs. Alice Weaver

Mr. Julius B. Anthony

I would like to give a special thank you to my parents

(Edward and Wanda Thomas) for always supporting me.

Author's Notes

This book was written to introduce early learners to colors and fruits. For emerging readers this book will help develop cognitive skills and expand vocabulary. Children can reach their highest learning potential simply by making books an integral part of their lives.

Yummy, Yummy in my Tummy!

Written by April Thomas   Illustrated by Cory Lampkin Jr.

Red Apples **are so sweet!**
Yummy, yummy in my tummy!

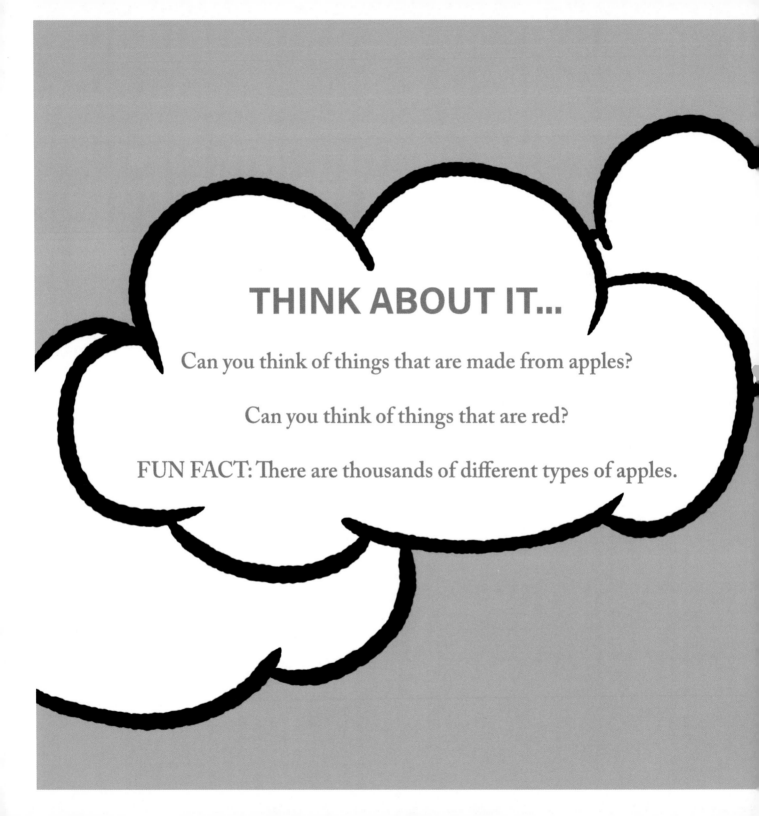

THINK ABOUT IT...

Can you think of things that are made from apples?

Can you think of things that are red?

FUN FACT: There are thousands of different types of apples.

Orange Oranges are so sweet!
Yummy, yummy in my tummy!

THINK ABOUT IT...

Can you think of things that begins with the letter "O"?

Can you think of things that are made from oranges?

FUN FACT: Orange peels have over four times the amount of fiber of the actual fruit.

Yellow Bananas are so sweet!
Yummy, yummy in my tummy!

THINK ABOUT IT...

Can you think of things that are yellow?

Can you think of things that begins with the letter "Y"?

FUN FACT: Bananas contain a lot of potassium.

**Green Pears are so sweet!
Yummy, yummy in my tummy!**

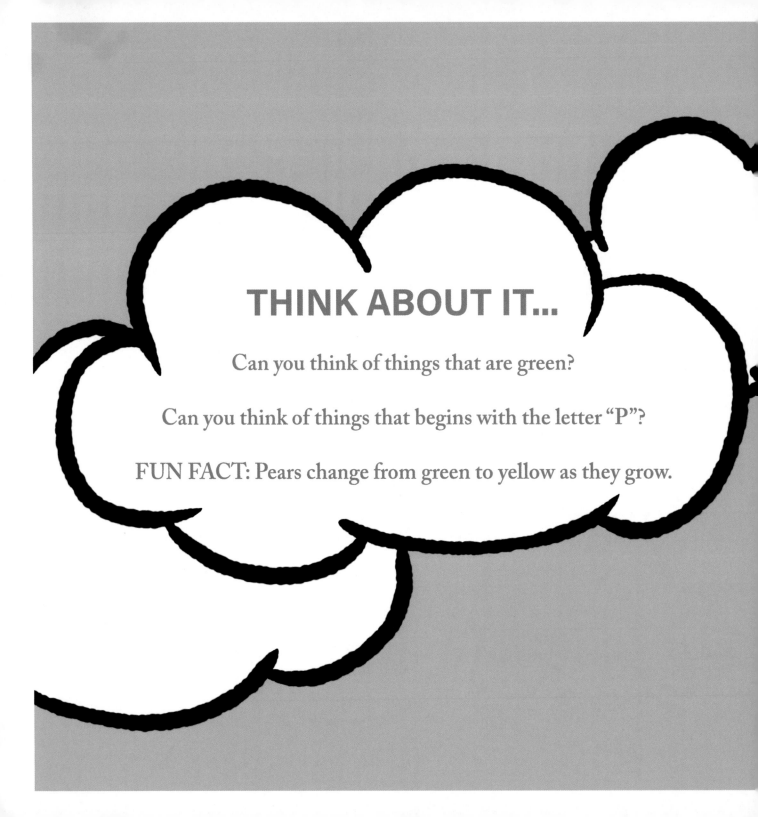

THINK ABOUT IT...

Can you think of things that are green?

Can you think of things that begins with the letter "P"?

FUN FACT: Pears change from green to yellow as they grow.

Blue Blueberries are so sweet!
Yummy, yummy in my tummy!

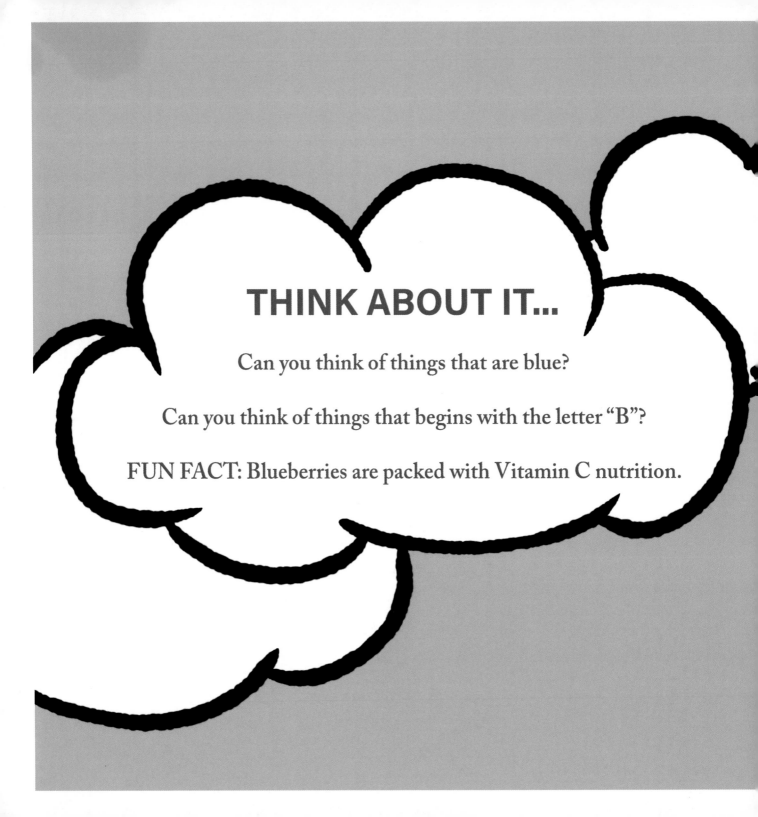

THINK ABOUT IT...

Can you think of things that are blue?

Can you think of things that begins with the letter "B"?

FUN FACT: Blueberries are packed with Vitamin C nutrition.

Purple Grapes are so sweet!
Yummy, yummy in my tummy!

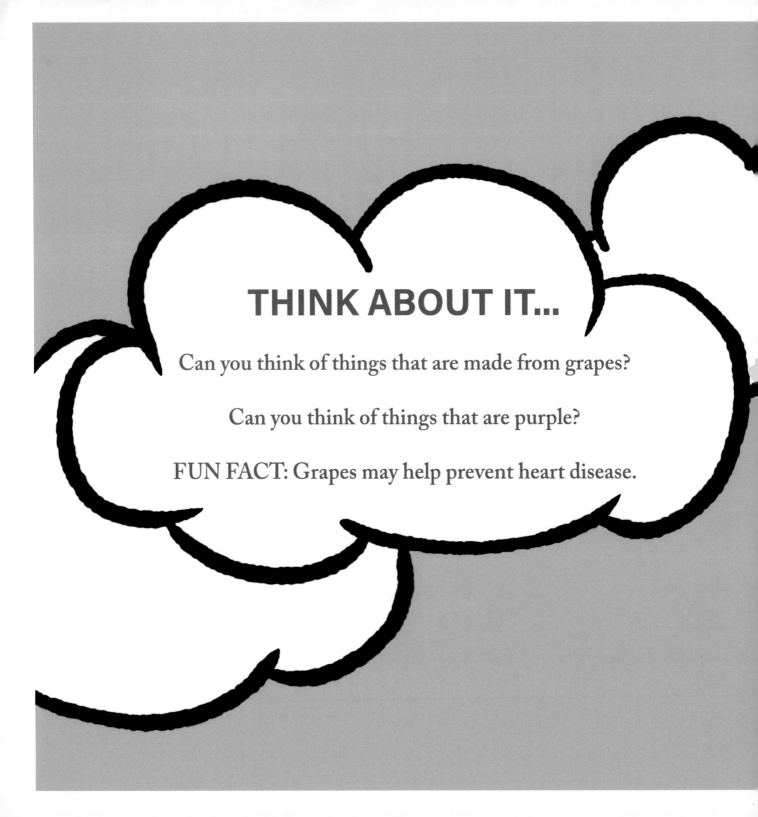

THINK ABOUT IT...

Can you think of things that are made from grapes?

Can you think of things that are purple?

FUN FACT: Grapes may help prevent heart disease.

**Pink Watermelons are so sweet!
Yummy, yummy in my tummy!**

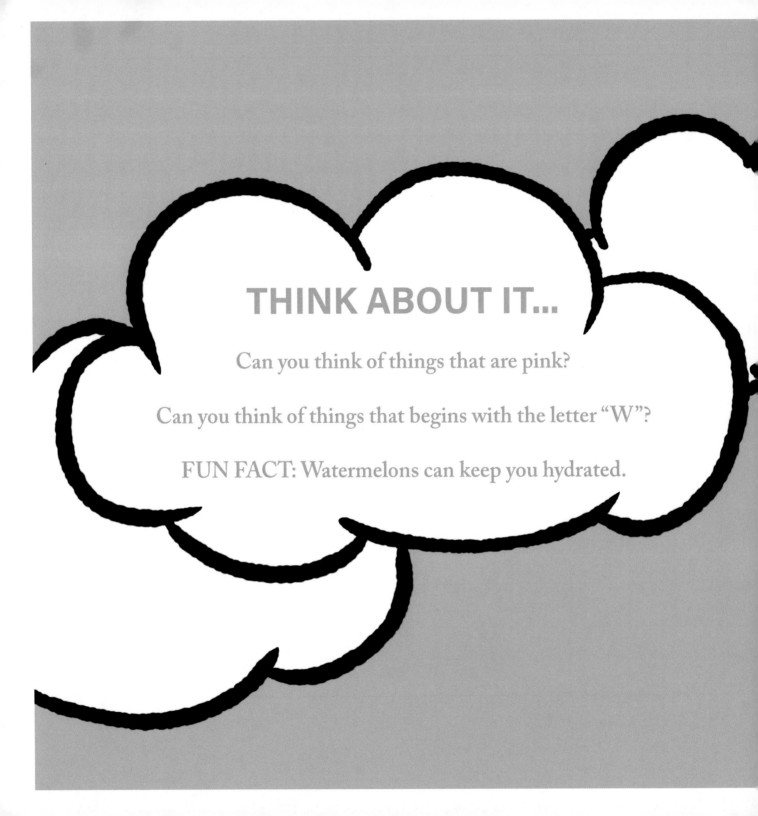

THINK ABOUT IT...

Can you think of things that are pink?

Can you think of things that begins with the letter "W"?

FUN FACT: Watermelons can keep you hydrated.

WORDS TO KNOW

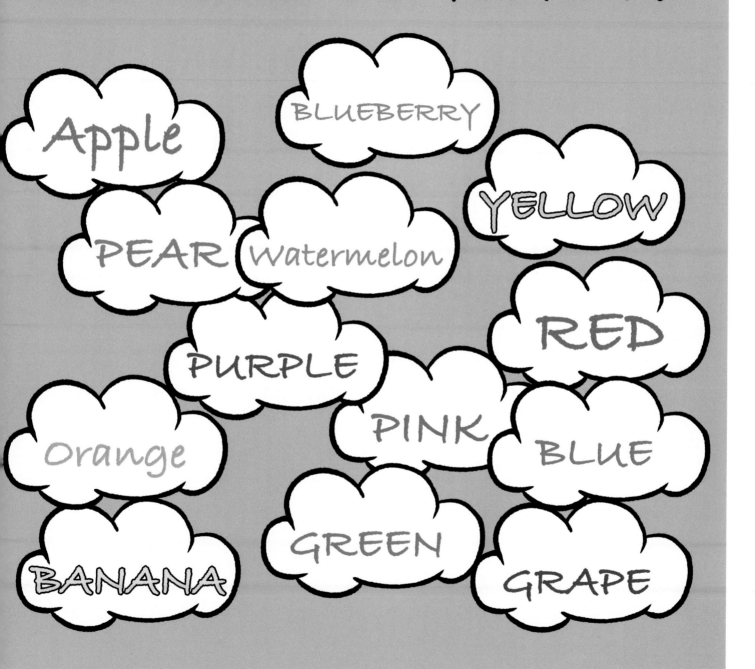

MEET THE AUTHOR

April Thomas has a Bachelors of Science in Early Childhood Education from Harris-Stowe State University in St. Louis, Missouri. She is currently an early childhood teacher in the St. Louis metropolitan area. April has a passion for children's literature. Her life goal is to create a nonprofit with the mission to ensure all children experience the power and joy of reading.

Made in the USA
Monee, IL
10 October 2020